A TREASURY
OF POETRY

A TREASURY OF POETRY

Poems inspired while
pursuing a purposeful life

W. Marie Giles

A Treasury of Poems
Published by Heart-in-Hands Enterprises
Copyright 2014 by W. Marie Giles

Library of Congress Control Number: 2014913710

ISBN: 978-0-9728944-3-2

Cover design: W. Marie Giles
Book layout design: W. Marie Giles

Printed in the United States of America

Dedication

This writing is dedicated to my family, friends, and all who cherish the reading and enjoyment of inspired poems.

OTHER BOOKS BY W. MARIE GILES

Open Your Mind, Open Your Heart: A collection of words of wisdom, heartfelt thoughts, and original poetry

Pay Attention To Your Life: Reflections on self-awareness and self-determination

Living Life With Conscious Intention: Key behaviors for enriching your life and the world we live in

Contents

Preface

I have long considered creating a collection of all my poems in a single book to share with those who would enjoy reading them. As I read through my collection, I decided to separate them into categories that reflect their meanings. I came up with these:

- Love
- Life
- Emotion
- Fate
- Beliefs
- Tragedy and Death
- Purpose
- Family
- Celebration

Many of the poems here are also included in my previous 3 books. Some, however, have never been published in any book prior to this one.

As I write each poem, I truly feel the emotions associated with them including, beauty, love, joy, sadness, depression, fear, wonder, curiosity, frustration, and many others reflecting the particular inspiration prompting the writing. These feelings flow through me, resulting in the poems you will read here.

It is my hope and intention that you will savor each word, sentence, thought, and inspiration included in each of the poems, knowing they are not merely written for my own sake. They were given to me to share with you.

"Everything has been thought of before, but the difficulty is to think of it again." -- Goethe

Acknowledgement

I wish to acknowledge my gratitude for God's insights on the true purpose of my life.

I wish to thank my family and friends for their confidence and interest in my writing projects over the past years, as well as their encouragement and support.

"To love and be loved is to feel the sun from both sides."   – David Viscott

About the Author

W. Marie Giles retired from the Federal Civil Service in the field of Information Technology where she advanced to senior management during her 30-year career.

Marie has been on a journey of self-discovery and self-improvement nearly all her life. She has come to realize the journey does not end, for "it is in the journey that you continue to improve your outlook and reach a higher level of fulfillment."

Marie is also the author *of Open Your Mind, Open Your Heart: A collection of words of wisdom, heartfelt thoughts*; *Pay Attention To Your Life: Reflections on self-awareness and self-determination;* and *Living Life With Conscious Intention: Key behaviors for enriching your life and the world we live in.*

"The most important thing a man can do with his life is to live it as himself."   -- Anonymous

Poems About Love

The Lesson

Fate steered us right,
Though pain to each is caused.
We must fight through it,
Until we arrive THERE.

THERE is where we belong.
A state, a place, with or without
The things we desire or the fears we face.

We BELONG together,
Though painful it may be.
A lesson is being taught
That we must learn -
Before we can arrive.

Open up and let the learning take place.
The journey slows to closed
Minds and hearts.

Come to me, take me to you.
Hold me close, touch me gently,
Speak kindly, look softly, and you'll see...
The Lesson is LOVE!

If

If I could say to you
What my heart has said to me,
I could put your mind at ease
And then our lives would be
Truly intertwined
As one
As we become
The soul of our very BEING.

If I could only make you see
That my life is you and me
Outside, inside, in between,
You, me, and everything.
Our hopes and dreams
The times we share,
The love we give,
The ways we care.
Opening our eyes and SEEING.

If I could give to you the things
That I think you deserve
I would soon exhaust my supply
And there would be no reserve.

For I think you should have
The World,
The sun, the moon, the stars,
Your girl,
Your one and only,
Your terribly lonely
Your life,
Your world,
Your family,
Your Sweet, Lady!

Without Words?

I cannot envision myself without our hope
Or expectation of communication.
For as long as we have been acquainted
This particular part of me absconds vacation.

To say you've grown to be
So very much a part of me
Is to understate the beauty
And importance of our greatest tree.

No, what you've come to mean to me
Is so very hard to explain
Without the aid of words and phrases
Which appear to me only in vain.

So many fine phrases are battling
Even now within my mind
To come forward and serve the purpose of
Not merely indicating to you the very importance of
this time.

Elaborating on this to you
Would not really be a most pressing thing to do.

See, what I'm trying to say is that
Our lives really changed when we met that fortunate
day.

To simply say I love you
Would nearly be enough;
To say I really need you is
Less that poetic "buff".

But then, to say I love you, need you, want you

with consideration attached—
And add affection – strive for your eternal presence -
Well words and emotion are very nearly evenly
matched.

Who can verbally express emotion so strong and
deep-seated as yours and mine?
It can only truly manifest itself with the help of the
endless and constant revolution of the wheels of time.

The Circle of Love

The circle of love is unbroken
Because we each proceed
To reach out to another
Whenever we see a need.

Should one decide to falter,
The next cannot move on.
He has no hand to hold him
Or push him further along.

Reach out to help another
Every day you live;
And someone else will help you
When it comes his time to give.

Don't let the circle be broken.
We all can use the love.
And remember that it all started
With the Glorious One above.

What You Mean To Me

A loving glance that tells me you still care;
Remembering the happy times we share;

A simple touch that says "I'm glad you're here."
A reassuring voice that allays my fear;

A confidence that says "I know you can."
A willingness to always lend a hand;

A tender kiss upon my lips each day;
As I must leave and go my separate way;

A smiling face to meet each workday's end;
A comforting and everlasting friend.

As time goes by revealing the mystery
Of life and love and all that's meant to be—
These things – and more – you'll always mean to me.

Within My Heart

Take my hand, come go with me,
And live within my heart.
As long as you remain there,
I know we'll never part.

The love we have was meant to be
For as long as there is air
For us to breathe as we begin
A life we promised to share.

The ups and downs, the good and bad
Will only serve to be
A source of strength and fortitude
For our new-formed family.

I'll take your hand, my precious one,
To you my heart I'll give;
Remain there within, my love,
For as long as we both shall live.

My One And Only Love

I think of you as roses red,
And sweet as fragrant dew,
That falls upon the earth at dawn,
And calls me close to you.

You are my one and only love,
To you I pledge my life.
My faith and honor are yours to keep,
For you my darling wife.

My Knight in Shining Armor

You are my knight in shining armor,
Ever ready when I call.
You've been with me through good and bad times,
Sickness, good health, and all.

And through the years we've grown together
Rich experiences beyond measure.
I wouldn't trade our life and time
For any material treasure.

To you, my knight, I pledge my heart
Along with all my love.
Our destiny, our fate intertwined
A union blessed from above.

Just The Two Of Us

When it was just the two of us,
We did a lot together.
It didn't matter – hot or cold -
Or whatever the weather.

We'd walk along a crowded street,
Holding each other's hands;
Oblivious to passers-by
No worries, no demands.

We'd laugh and joke and jump for joy,
Whenever we came near
The place where we would always know
There was nothing to fear.

For in the arms of the one you love
Is comfort – safe and warm.
And feelings of a life and love
Free from hurt and harm.

When We First Met

When we first met
You knocked me off my feet!
The last 30 years have been
Even more of a treat.

We've shared the good
Sometimes the bad
And Oh My Love
What a time we've had.

Raising kids
And working hard
We put our trust
And faith in our Dear Lord.

This day is so very special
To share with you my love
An angel sent directly
To me from Heaven above.

In another 30 years
I pray that we will be
Still living this beautiful dream
I for you and you for me.

Always and forever
Leaving each other never.

The Years

The years have gone by
So fast it seems
While we were so busy
Fulfilling our dreams.

Raising kids
And busy with careers –
We barely took time
To count the years.

Now here we are
At number 27 –
Still loving and living
A page from Heaven.

The next round of years
Will bring joy and hope,
Though we must contend
With whatever the slope.

The love we've shared –
Year after year –
Will keep us moving forward
Without reservations or fear.

Love One Another

"There will be wars and rumors of wars."
That's what we were taught long ago.
When this world as we know it comes to an end
As many countries are making that so.

The fighting against one another continues
As power plays and threats come to past.
No one knows what these actions will bring
Or how long they are likely to last.

If we could realize we are all God's children --
Brothers and Sisters one and all,
This violence and cruelty surely could stop
As we take time to answer His call.

Love one another as He loves us all.
He sacrificed His son for our sins.
If we can appreciate such a massive act of love
We will know where that love begins.

Love, like charity, begins at home
We then spread it more widely from there –
Giving of ourselves as we move through our lives
Expecting nothing in return for such care.

By taking more time to spread the peace
And help others try and do the same,
We'll not only be living the life He meant for us,
We'll be doing it in His Holy name.

Our Dreams

Dreams realized is what we have
Over all these years together.
A relationship that*s strong and true,
Throughout any type of weather.

This special day is ours to share,
As we were joined as one.
Pledging always to honor and cherish
For many more years to come.

"Imagination was given to man to compensate him for what he is not; a sense of humor, to console him for what he is."

-- The Wall Street Journal

Poems About Life

> *"In the book of life, the answers aren't in the back."*
> **-- Charlie Brown**

Optimism/Pessimism

Optimism is its own reward.
It's much like when we draw a lucky card.
It helps us realize our hopes and dreams,
And the task-at-hand is easier than it seems.

Pessimism seeks to bring us down,
And makes our face a constant, gloomy frown.
It strips us of our hopes and dreams,
And takes away our drive and self-esteem.

Just realize the choice is yours to make.
Be careful that it's not a big mistake.
For one will make your life a living hell.
The other will keep you happy and living well.

Which do you choose?

Boundaries

Boundaries are necessary
To keep our kids from harm.
We set them up like sand-to-sea
So they feel safe and warm.

They may roar and may rebel
But we must stand steadfast.
The lessons we teach today
Are truly the ones that last.

Boundaries are also set
To keep us in our place,
And help us know the way to go
In returning to our base.

We sometimes try to reach beyond
The line He drew for us;
And He is there to let us know
That all we need is trust.

Sometimes He may allow us
To stretch beyond that line;
This only serves to help us see
His truth is most divine.

For when the right time comes along
To move beyond His mark
We will know the journey upon which
He leads us to embark.

Undisputed

He lives inside his head all day
And rarely sleeps at night;
Keeps to himself and speaks few words
For survival he will fight.

Inside his world, he is the champ –
An undisputed fact.
Each challenger will realize
It's more than just an act.

Outside his world, he's not well-known;
For who out there would care
About a man condemned to hell
Where violence is not rare?

A man who lives inside his head
Never fears the day
When someone else can take him down
And take his crown away.

Until that day, he stays within
With a discipline you can't refute.
He's the champ and this, for sure,
Is a fact you can't dispute.

Is That Really Me?

Who was I?
Where did I go?
I've searched and searched
Still I don't know.

Where was I?
What did I do?
Did you know me?
Did I know you?

Daughter, sister, cousin, friend,
Mother, wife, all I've been.
All these roles I've had to play,
Year in, year out, day-by-day.

The time has passed before I knew it,
The ones I am and have been to do it,
All within a short life span,
While being held in the palm of His hand.

Everyone Has a Story to Tell

Everyone has a story to tell.
It's what we're all about.
Our life and times kept safe inside.
Do we want to let it out?

Ordinary or extraordinary,
We can weigh them all the same.
For we are all born and we all die
You don't have to know their name.

When you see a stranger on the street,
Don't pass without a thought
Of how they've lived and who they are
Or what their life's about.

Pain and suffering or joy of life—
It's all right there to see.
If we look past the outer core
We'll think, "They're just like me."

Life Through Books

She's always buying books to read
She has a desperate need
To learn all she can of life
And cure the world of strife.

Most of the time she feels content
As books are such good friends.
But reality strikes and brings her back
To a life of constant amends.

Energy's up and then it's down
How does she cope with it
And all the things she tries to do
To keep herself well-fit.

Her life is split between so much
She tries so hard to please
Her family, friends, and everyone
Until she's ill-at-ease.

Heart and mind just open up
To let hurt and happiness in
Sometimes it's good, sometimes it's bad
But with it she does contend.

So off she goes to get a book
To answer what she asks
It's what she knows will do the trick
And put her back on task.

Life

We think we have it all figured out.
We think we know what life is all about.

Thinking that we know just what to do
"Live and Learn" – but is that really true?

For some this is easy
And life is good.
For others nothing seems to turn out
As it should.

Some are living life from day-to-day
Others seem to constantly go astray.

Still many others tend mainly to look ahead
While others simply wish that they were dead.

Such is life...

Another Chapter

As you complete this chapter in life's book
Take some time to have another look

At all the ones that you have put behind
And think about just how they did unwind.

Sit back, relax – recall the happy times;
Never erase those memories from your mind.

Do not forget the times when things were sad;
Lest you forget there's always good and bad.

You may have had some hard times in the past;
But there's no reason why they have to last.

No one said it's easy growing up.
Survivors, by their nature, must be tough.

Well you have shown the world that you can make it.
Whatever life is giving, you can take it.

The book of life is many chapters long,
Filled with stories of the weak and strong.

The time is now to choose the one you'll be
Have faith and hope – it all works out –
You'll see!

Tender Moments

A mother's heart holds lots of Tender
Moments which she gives
To those for whom she loves and cares
Each and every day she lives.

A father's strong and tough demeanor
Won't readily reveal
The Tender Moments within his heart
That he safely conceals.

A child brings us Tender Moments
When born into the world.
They give us a measure of hope and joy
Whether it's a boy or a girl.

Tender Moments can be revealed
In efforts to save a life.
They're evident in words spoken
Between a husband and wife.

Tender Moments are what we need
With them we can't go wrong.
They get us through the bad times
And keep the good times strong.

Tender Moments are what we make
When we show others we care;
Reaching out and comforting,
Opening our hearts to share.

Tender Moments warm our hearts
And help us through our days.
Whether they are given or received
They work in wondrous ways.

So share a Tender Moment
With a loved-one or a friend.
And let them know how much you care
Over and over again.

Seeing Yourself As Others Do

Seeing yourself differently than others do
Can limit your success.
'Cause others see the good and bad,
Which you might not assess.

To see their views, look inside,
Where all your secrets rest.
Be honest with yourself and them.
Put yourself to the test.

Seeing yourself as others do
May change your point of view,
Your attitude, your outlook,
The things you say and do.

The **way** you say and hear things
May also change, it's true.
And how you view the world, at large,
May seem to be brand new.

Don't hesitate, don't be afraid
To take this chance to know,
How this small step can change your life
And the direction you choose to go.

Once you have come to terms
With who you really are,
The rest will fall right into place
And your life will be richer, by far.

Find The Courage To Find Your Voice

If you have something "real" to say
That others may want to hear,
Find a way to cast aside
Your reluctance and your fear.

You'll never know how well you'll do
Until you've given it a try.
Don't sit inside your man-made shell
Until the day you die.

What you'll say could change a life,
Or bring a bright, big smile.
It could even mend a broken heart,
Or touch the soul of a child.

So get prepared, take the chance,
And let your heart be your guide.
Open your mouth – the words will flow,
You'll be really glad you tried.

True Meaning

Dear Lord, help us to understand
The true meaning of it all;
As we proceed throughout our lives
When we rise and when we fall.

Help us know that you are there,
Whether things are good or rough.
Fill our minds with ways to "make it",
Whenever life gets tough.

Lord, touch our hearts and let us know,
Through the sunshine and the rain,
The true meaning of a particular thing
Is that it is never, ever in vain.

What Matters Most

A physical body, worn or torn,
Matters less and less you see;
Than an open mind and a caring heart
And who we were born to be.

Each and every one of us
Was placed here for a reason.
We must continue to seek and search
For our own individual season.

What matters, then, the most, dear friend,
Is that we realize,
That our true purpose in this life
Is filled with sacrifice.

We may not always get the things
We pray for from above.
What matters most is that our God
Has ways to show His love.

He gives us life with special meaning
When we're willing to pay attention.
He keeps on nudging us with hope
Despite our own dissension.

Sooner or later we start to see
Just what His messages mean,
If we have faith and stand steadfast
Believing in things not yet seen.

It's Your Life

Your **body** is a temple
Given by God to you.
Treat it with the utmost respect
And your ailments will be few.

Your **mind** should not be wasted
On useless, idle fare.
You may awaken one morning,
And find it's no longer there.

Nurture a clear, clean **spirit**
And seek to be close to God.
As long as you keep this in mind,
From Him you will never, ever part.

Temper your heated **emotions**
For God has given to you
The power of careful, thoughtful response
In everything you do.

Attention to these four dimensions,
When practiced day-by-day,
Will help you lead your very best life
In every possible way.

It's Never Too Late

It's never too late to live your life
The way you think you can.
It's never too late to let the world
See that you have a plan.

Start using all the lessons
You've learned year after year.
It's never too late to stand up and shout
"Hey, World, know that I am here!"

Once you can accept your life
For its true purpose – whatever the call --
You'll see the world take notice
And you'll forever be standing tall.

The most important thing to know --
As you decide to proceed --
Your life is just what you make it.
Believe this and you'll succeed.

Sometimes it takes more courage
Than you ever believed you had.
Sometimes you have to "just do it",
And say, "That was not so bad!"

Now why not try to find out
What's really holding you back?
And once you do you'll notice
It's nothing that you lack.

For all you need to move forward,
Has already been given to you.
Just know that the choice is yours
And that will get you through.

It's never too late to play this game
No matter what others say.
And no matter the discouragement,
There's no better time than today.

Helping Others

When you reach out to others,
And help them in their plight,
You become a better person
In dealing with your own personal fight.

They really will appreciate
The tireless things you do,
In getting them back on a track
That eases their pain, too.

So never stop your giving
And helping others strive
To get their lives together
And continue to feel alive.

No matter what you do or say,
It's still the only way.
So reach out to another,
And fulfill your purpose today.

Double Digit

I'm 10, I'm 10!
No longer in
The single-digit age.

I'm 10, I'm 10
I've reached the top
The world is now my stage!

A Major Milestone

You've been waiting and waiting,
Your whole life through,
To get older and older,
And become a freer you.

You've been seeking and searching,
For much of that time,
For more knowledge and wisdom,
And your own day to shine.

For you, 21
Represents this milestone,
To do as you please,
Feel in control, on your own.

As you continue to grow older,
And we hope wiser, still,
We pray that you'll remember,
It all comes with a bill.

For you have to pay dues,
To get what you deserve.
You must seek a higher order,
Of the Master you serve.

Nothing is gained
Without giving, you'll find.
And nothing is granted
Without payment in kind.

So never stop growing,
And never stop yearning.
Your life will be richer
If you never stop learning.

Our Lighthouse

You've been our bright light guiding us
Through calm and stormy times
You never, never faltered,
Always keeping us in mind.

The advice you gave was needed
We knew just when to call.
You never, ever tired of giving
A cheerful response to all.

We hope you'll return for a moment
Visiting us time and again
So we can catch another glimpse
Of a light that will never wane.

You've been our lighthouse beacon,
Shining ever so bright.
We'll miss your clear, rescuing beam
As we continue on our plight.

Negative Energy and Positive Thoughts

There's so much negative energy
Existing in our lives today.
Do you find yourself just wishing
You could make it all go away?

But, where could you possibly send it
Without it ending up somewhere
In someone else's peaceful domain
Causing them the same despair?

You pray and pray for some relief
From having to contend
With so much negative energy
Never, ever seeing an end.

You try to have some positive thoughts
To help get through the day.
But someone always comes along
Bringing negative thoughts your way.

You tell yourself you have to choose
a happy, grateful stance
To keep from being affected by
The negativity trance.

You must keep your mind attuned
To Positive, more pleasant things,
To get you through those trying times
And help your heart to sing.

Try a positive tune and a happy dance,
Knowing He holds you near.
Listen to what He tells you.
It's all He wants you to hear.

Always Continue

Always continue to reach for the stars,
In all you choose to do.
Always continue to pursue a life
That's honest, simple, and true.

Always continue to pay attention
To the things that really matter.
Always continue to use your gifts
To make life a little better.

Put Others First

"Do the right thing."
Is easy to say,
If you are the one who is
Getting your way.

It may be harder
And harder to do
If the winner of the struggle
Is other than you.

Looking past yourself, you see
Is what's called for with this.
Thinking of others surely could be
What is first on your list.

When you become tempted
To always put yourself first
Try thinking, praying,
Or reading a verse,

From God's great collection
Of how we should live.
It's the ultimate guide
Which makes it easier to give.

Commitment

Commit yourself to the things in your life
And don't fear going the distance.
Keep your mind ever focused and ready
And never lose your persistence.

Stick with your goals and don't let them go.
Keep moving ever forward and then you will know
Commitment requires that you weather some storms
Many ups and downs outside of life's norms.

As long as you have faith
Keeping God as your guide,
You won't fear risking failure
As you keep a constant stride.

It's Time To Let Go

It's time to let go and leave this era,
To do more of the things you please.
No more pondering throughout each day
Go and seek a life of ease.

You deserve to know the feeling –
And experience true joy and peace.
Commit yourself to doing good deeds,
Reflecting your true purpose without cease.

You'll leave behind a legacy
Of your true and lasting essence,
Which many will remember you for --
Having been honored by your presence.

Each path in life has a beginning and end
To live, cherish, and hold dear –
Remember both the good and bad,
Moving on to the next given tier.

Say "So long", without regret,
Letting all know you still care.
Then make your exit to continue your journey
Free of a load you no longer have to bear.

The Project Manager Hat

Put on a Project Manager Hat
And see what it entails.
Find out what you need to do –
Get all the vital details.

A PM's job is not so hard
It just requires a lot of work.
Take on this role and commit yourself,
You may become an expert.

But, regardless if you do or don't,
That's really not what's key.
Your taking this important step
Is what we'd like to see.

Take your Own Advice

When you get confused about what to do
Try taking your own advice --
The words you preach or teach to others
Don't hesitate or even think twice.

If your advice is good enough
For others to accept and take,
Why not try taking it yourself
And give your wisdom a fair shake.

"Practice what you preach." And "What's good for the
goose..."
Are phrases which come to mind.
When you give advice for others to follow,
Your example should be along the same lines.

"How you spend your time is more important than how you spend your money. Money mistakes can be corrected, but time is gone forever."   -- David B. Norris

Poems About Emotion

> *"I don't want to be at the mercy of my emotions. I want to use them, to enjoy them, and to dominate them."*
> **-- Oscar Wilde**

Stop the Anger!
Kindness
Depression
Sadness
More Than Just Your Presence
Sunshine and Rain

Stop the Anger!

Angry woman,
Cool your heels.
Count to ten.
See how it feels.

Angry man,
Love your wife.
Give her a hug.
Change your life.

Angry children,
Stop the fuss.
Obey your parents.
Do what you must.

Kindness

Kindness costs you nothing,
Yet, it can buy more than silver, gold, or even money.

Kindness can only be given, never taken –
Once received, it becomes a torch to be passed on.

Kindness is a blanket that warms the heart.

Kindness can heal the hurt
Or ease the pain;
Soothe the soul
Or cool the flames;
Bring a smile
Or dry a tear;
Brighten a mood
Or calm a fear.

Kindness can come from stranger or friend,
Small acts or big ones, all to the same end.

You can give and receive kindness and so can I.
If more of us give it, more will receive it.

Don't wait another minute,
It's simple to do
You to me, me to you.

Try a smile or lend a hand.
Give a ride or share what you can.

Kiss your kids or hug your love.
Give a wink or mend a glove.
Kindness makes a difference!

Depression

Do you ever get so depressed
You cannot do a thing?
You try and try to shake it
But it's almost like a dream.

You try to wake yourself up
With good and positive thoughts
But your mind and body won't react
The way you think they ought.

You'll have to wait until it passes
And returns control to you.
So reconcile yourself to that
And soon a light shines through.

Many times it's over
Not long after it starts.
Other times it lasts so long
It tears into your heart.

Try to maintain hopeful thoughts
To send it on its way --
Knowing you will wake up soon
Ready to face another day!

Sadness

There's a sadness that sometimes surrounds me,
I can't seem to control.
I try real hard to reject it,
But it seems to take its toll.

I try to think of more positive things
To make my heart feel good.
But that doesn't always help me
As much as I think it should.

Lower and lower I seem to sink,
Engulfed by doom and dread.
What is this thing that comes over me?
What must I do instead?

Prayer is the one sure thing
That helps the hurt or pain;
And asking for a ray of hope
To get me through the rain.

Soon, before I know it
He shines His light on me
I release my burden unto Him
And I know He will set me free.

More Than Just Your Presence

We need more than just their presence
And the things that THEY adore --
Like all the cleaning, cooking, laundry,
And a host of other chores.

We need someone to hold us
And let us know they care;
Not just about the things we do
But the character we bear.

We're the women of today
With a flair of our Mothers before.
We're strong yet vulnerable beings
With duty at our core.

We work so hard to care for them
And rarely ever complain.
We deal with lack of gratitude
And behave as if we're tame.

We need a pair of good strong arms,
To hold us close and tight
And a caring voice to reassure us
That things will be all right.

We need support in all we do
Acknowledgement of our worth,
Occasional compliments and a "Thank You"
Could be just like Heaven on Earth!

Sunshine and Rain

Sometimes there's so much rain,
We can barely get through the day.
Other times, as we enjoy the sunshine,
We can barely find words to say.

But then there are times we experience
Both the sunshine and the rain –
A balancing act sent straight from God,
To get us through both joy and pain.

Knowing that each is needed,
To reveal His way to us.
There can hardly be one without the other,
You know this if you keep your trust.

So try real hard to understand,
What He's trying to let us know.
There will always be good and bad on Earth,
That's how it was meant to go.

We all must tolerate some rain at times,
To know the difference, you see.
So whenever the sunshine is sent our way,
We can welcome it with glee.

"Stormy weather is what man needs from time to time to remind him he's not in charge of anything."   -- Bill Vaughn

Poems About Fate

> *"Accept the things to which fate binds you, and love the people with whom fate brings you together, but do so with all your heart."*
> — **Marcus Aurelius, Meditations**

Fate

I see your hurt;
I feel your pain;
It's like the storm
With all the rain.

Dry your eyes and lift your head;
Stand up tall and don't you dread.
There are brighter days if you just wait.
Go to your destiny – meet your fate.

For Everything A Reason

Her heart aches for want of arms to hold her
Simply because she needs a hug...

She longs to hear kind words to let her know that
she does not cause the anger...

She walks on eggshells just so she does not disturb
others
While they are preoccupied...

Her house is full, yet she feels all alone.
Their wants have over-shadowed their needs.

They are ruled by these desires, yet
Enslaved by their fears of each other.

How long will it last?
When will her family start to be?
Was it really meant to be?

God does not make mistakes!
Keep searching for the reason for as long as it takes.

It's ALWAYS there.

Lessons Learned?

When we are young we think we know it all.
No one can tell us we're not ten feet tall.
We think the world owes us so much more
Than we are willing to work or even pay for.

As we get older, we remain a bit misguided;
Believing we can get through life undecided
About the things we must do in order to succeed.
We still refuse to listen and take heed.

Still older yet, we try to act so wise.
Hoping others won't see it in our eyes –
The fact that we did not each opportunity seize
When we were younger and doing as we please.

You look around for someone else to blame –
To those who have achieved fortune and fame.
You try to say "No one gave me a chance."
But it was you who simply refused to dance.

Life is full of lessons each and every day.
It's up to you to learn along the way.
An open mind is Oh so very key
If you are to fulfill your destiny.

A President for All of America

We may never have been so full of pride
As what we are feeling tonight.
America has cast an important vote
And, yes we got it right!

A President for all of us
Is all we've ever wanted.
A man after our own beliefs –
A loyal American – undaunted.

We have a duty as Americans
To respect and not impede.
We have a responsibility
To support and follow his lead.

President-elect Obama we salute you
With our hands and within our hearts,
And pledge to you right here, right now,
In earnest to do our parts.

Success to you on the road ahead,
Good Luck, Godspeed, All the Best.
We stand behind you with strong support
And loyalty – whatever the test!

A President For All Of America II

The American people have spoken again
This time even more loud and clear.
A President after our own values and heart
For the issues we hold so dear.

A Gracious God made this possible,
With the prayers of all those who care.
Barack Obama deserves this chance
To keep moving FORWARD and get us there.

We believe in you, Mr. President,
Even more than 4 years ago.
Let's go the distance together, again,
And prove we can all make it so!

Presidential Inauguration 2013

I was moved by the President's speech,
On his second inauguration,
After taking the oath to serve and preserve
The legacy of our great nation.

He spoke of how we were created
Endowed by His sacred might,
With life, liberty, and the pursuit of happiness,
And the Declaration gives us this right.

His speech addressed the rights of all –
No matter the path they pursue.
We are all given this opportunity --
That includes me and all of you.

As you follow this current President,
Try to find a way to measure,
With genuine commitment and support,
The true values that we all treasure.

For he is truly a blessing to us,
No matter our faith, color, or race.
His intention remains to serve us all,
As we ponder what he must now face.

Your Place To Shine

Your place to shine is where you are,
Today -- right here, right now.
The many things that are meant for you
Will come to past somehow.

Don't try to rush the course of your life
That was given to you to live.
Just set your sights on who you are
And the gifts you were meant to give.

I Am

I am who I am
No matter what you say.
You can look at my face
Or you can look away.

I know who I am
No matter what you think.
Like a chip that floats
Or sandbags that sink.

The Hand of God

You cannot force the Hand of God
No matter how hard you pursue it.
If there is something meant to be
He'll be there to bring you through it.

He lifts you up when you are down,
Yet brings you to your knees.
However He directs your plight,
He's there and never leaves.

So trust that He is All-knowing
Of our problems big and small.
He takes great care of each of us,
Delivering blessings and lessons to all.

Poems About Beliefs

> *"Every mental act is composed of doubt and belief,*
> *but it is belief that is the positive, it is belief*
> *that sustains thought and holds the world together."*
> — Søren Kierkegaard

A Need to Know?

I wish that I could plainly see
All the things in store for me.
My hopes and dreams and all those things --
The opportunities that living brings.

My family, friends, and all they need;
The things that make us follow and lead.

Should I pass on before it's done,
I'll not regret a single one
Of all the things that helped me know
The way that I was meant to go.

Angels

I believe in Angels.
I can feel them all around.
They're up above, in the air,
And also on the ground.

Angels help us deal with life.
They help us see the light
Throughout the dark when we can't see
They get us through the night.

If someone comes to lend a hand
Whenever you're in need,
You can know, be sure of this,
It was an Angel, indeed.

Angels come in many forms
It might just be your pet.
Or they may look like you or me,
Your doctor or the vet.

Be careful how you look at life
And all those that you meet.
Don't be so quick to challenge things
There is an Angel at your feet.

With Each New Day

As I am blessed with each new day,
I have a talk with God.
And thank Him for the gift of life
That He chose to impart.

I thank Him for His company
Throughout my busy day.
I thank Him for the discipline
That He has sent my way.

I thank Him for my health, strength,
Courage, and well-being.
I thank Him for necessities
Such as walking, talking, seeing.

I thank Him for the mind not wasted
On idle, useless things.
I thank Him for my patience and
The good things that it brings.

I thank Him for the kind exchange
Between me and the stranger.
I thank Him for the many times
That I was slow to anger.

And when my day begins again,
I say another prayer.
I thank God for the loving ways
That He shows me He cares.

Good and Bad Times

When times are bad, look to the sky;
Then you can hold your head up high;
And know that things will work out right,
Never out of mind, never out of sight.

When times are good, bow down your head,
Each night before you go to bed.
Give thanks to God for all He's done
And how He takes care of His own.

Prayer for Sons

Dear Lord, hold him in your hands
And let him make good choices.
Keep him safe from hurt and harm
While hearing the heavenly voices.

Let his will be strongly set
Where he will do his best;
Always ready, always prepared
For any trial or test.

Let the good within his heart
Shine through any mask.
And may he know that you are there
With him through every task.

Hope and Faith

Having hope is important,
Because we know that the Lord
Will preserve our faith and fortitude
As long as we do our part.

We must reach out to others
Giving them kindness and thought
And continue to maintain hope
That God will not leave us distraught.

In the face of disaster and devastation,
When things look hopeless and grim,
We wonder and cry, "Why us 'O Lord?"
But we continue to have faith in Him.

Hope is a critical part of faith –
Praying and wishing without knowing.
If faith is believing in things not yet seen
Then hope is what keeps us going.

We were granted the ability to hope
So our faith could remain without waver.
Even when we don't get what we hoped for,
Our faith keeps us strong and in His favor.

He Is In Control

No matter the job assigned to me
My work for the Lord will always be
At the center of my life in every action I take
In my heart of hearts and every move I make.

No one on Earth controls my fate
My destiny is determined from above.
He has me in his loving sight
And He showers me with His love.

Not one of us down here below
Can control what happens to us.
The Lord Jesus Christ is at the wheel
His decisions we can always trust.

We know He has us in His hands
Our faith tells us this much.
Keep hoping and believing that things will work out
You'll know it when you feel His touch.

All I Need

God will give me all I need
And show me what to do.
Although I get impatient,
He always gets me through.

The courage I need for moving forward
Is there, without a doubt.
Every act He prompts me to take,
I never wonder about.

He keeps my best interest at hand
With the highest level of love –
Casting down His wisdom and care,
From His glorious throne above.

God's Way

The Good Lord has His reasons
For all we do and say.
He points us in the right direction,
And leads us on our way.

If we complain about our life,
And ask Him why it's so,
He gently whispers His message to us
And shows us what we don't know.

All events throughout our lives,
Are colored with God's great pen.
He paints each chapter and every scene
From our beginning to the very end.

So if you question God's decisions,
Just know it'll be okay –
As long as you keep your trust in Him,
And know it's always His Way.

Happy Pills?

Don't wish for a magic, happy pill,
To help when you are down.
Just place your trust and faith in God,
He'll always be around.

He lifts us up, raising us high
To see what He wants us to see.
He makes His plans within our lives
To become what He wants us to be.

He guides us in reaching out
To help others find their way.
He gives us special praises and prayers
To say what He wants us to say.

When you search for happiness and joy,
There is no magic pill.
Only God, our Lord and Master
To give us all our fill.

The Light

You are the light unto my paths
To shine wherever I go.
No matter how far I venture,
You'll always let me know.
That you are there to comfort me
And shield me from hurt and pain;
To get me through the trying times,
The sunshine and the rain.

Take Courage

Take courage, my child,
Be of good cheer.
The Lord our God
Is always near.

No matter your plight,
He'll get you through,
In sickness and health,
He's always with you.

Stand up tall,
And always stay strong.
Give it your best
And you'll never go wrong.

"You can easily judge the character of a man by how he treats those who can do nothing for him."   -- Anonymous

Poems About Tragedy and Death

> *"You get tragedy where the tree, instead of bending, breaks."* -- **Ludwig Wittgenstein**
>
> *"The act of dying is one of the acts of life."*
> **-- Marcus Aurelius**

My Time Is Done
My Reward
Will I Be Missed?
We're All They Have Left
God's Will
A Letter From Heaven
An Old Soul
War for Peace
"...We Got Him"
The Columbia Seven
Farewell to Mattie
Farewell, Whitney
Thoughts on Hurricane Ivan
In Your Memory
Remembering
Coping With Life and Death

My Time Is Done

My time on Earth was what it was meant to be;
No more or less than anyone's, you see.
When we are born, our time is already set;
No matter what we do or say, that is all we get.

For some it may be minutes;
For others a few days or even years.
Whatever we are given,
We must welcome it with cheers.

No matter how many or few,
Life still goes too fast;
So whatever you choose to do with yours,
Try to leave something that will last.

For me, I leave you memories
Of how I tried to live,
With love and care for you and others
And all I tried to give.

So grieve for me if you must,
But not too long, dear one.
For if you believe and trust in God,
You'll know my time here is done.

My Reward

Today, I see my death as a wonderful reward,
As my Lord brings me closest to His heart.

I'm finally going home to take my rest,
Knowing now that I have done my best.

I realized my purpose in life early on,
The reason to this world that I was born.

I was chosen by the Lord above,
To touch the lives of those I know and love,
In a way that would stay with them forever,
And help them all to reach a higher level.

My work was fulfilling and sometimes took its toll,
While I pressed on to reach this final goal.

And now that I have given it my all,
I know at last that I have heard the call,
Telling me it's time to pass the torch,
And stand relieved of this, my final watch.

I know you all will grieve and cry for me.
But just remember how I came to be --
Living in this place for this brief time --
And keep this memory in your heart and mind.

(For Jackie)

Will I Be Missed?

Will I be missed when I am gone?
Will anyone cry for me?
For all the things that I have done
And all I tried to be?

Will they soon forget my name
And then dismiss the time
That I existed on this earth
And the deeds I left behind?

Or will they sing – rejoice for me
'Cause I tried to live a life
That helped to ease this ailing world
Of a little stress and strife?

Sometimes I wonder if I've done
What I came here to do.
And when I pray and ask the Lord,
He lets me know what's true.

For all that I have done and seen
It matters still, you see,
That I have made a lasting mark
And many will weep for me.

We're All They Have Left

As children close their eyes at night
And say their little prayer,
They know that when the morning comes,
Their family will still be there.

If, when the sun comes up again,
And all is as they asked,
They breathe a sigh of sweet relief
That things are still intact.

But, if they wake and no one's there
Whose face they recognize,
They turn their heads, squeeze real tight,
Then re-open their eyes.

Their hearts will sink and despair will grip
Their mind, body, and soul,
As they realize they've been left alone
With no loved ones to hold.

Now we the rest must care enough
For those suffering this ill.
We're all they have and God above
Has given us His will.

So take a hand and lead them on
– They have a lifetime to try
And make the best of this tragedy
They'll relive as time goes by.

For all our lives have now been touched
By such a senseless act;
But hand-in-hand, united we stand,
We'll make the journey back.

[Written in memory of the children left behind as a result of
September 11, 2001]

God's Will

If there was any other way
Your dear one would still be here
To comfort you and care for you
And calm all of your fears.

But God has put a will in place
Neither you nor I can change.
He also makes us strong enough
To suffer through hurt and pain.

Remember all the times you've shared
And let that comfort you.
Think of what your loved one would
Have wanted you to do.

It may seem now the time you had
Was too short to comprehend.
You wonder why it had to be
Such a quick and sudden end.

But keep your trust and faith in God
And know that He is near.
Just like your loved-one's spirit
Which you will always hold dear.

A Letter From Heaven

I was given a little time
Down there on God's green earth
He set the time for me to leave
Even before my birth.

He's giving you a little more time
So you can let others know
The Lord has all our plans in His hands
It's true, He told me so.

He controls the sun and moon,
The stars and all the rain.
And sometimes He will put us there
With lots and lots of pain.

Not because He doesn't care
Our teachings tell us that.
His sacrifice was the greatest of all
No one can argue the fact.

I know you do not understand
How God could let this be.
I knew the moment He called my name
He had a better place for me.

The pain and all the suffering
In my human form are gone.
But, Mom, I just need you to know
I'll never leave you alone.

I will visit with you from time-to-time
Throughout every single day
You may see and feel me there
Although not in a physical way.

Just look around and witness
God's miracles, great and small.
I just may be there in the midst
A helper at His call.

I'll always love you, Dearest Mom,
And cherish our times forever.
Until we meet again, in Heaven,
My Spirit will leave you never.

An Old Soul

An old soul has left us
And taken her place with God
We will sorely miss her.
But our memories will not depart.

She inspired us to live our lives
Without malice or regret --
Always showing us that, with her,
What you see is what you get.

We always embraced her candor,
Her humor and her grit;
And so many times she charmed us
With her knowledge, wisdom, and wit.

The inspiration she gave to us
Will live on in times to come.
This lets us know, deep in our hearts,
She was truly a chosen one.

"Good-bye" is not the phrase to use;
"See you later" is a better one.
For our faith tells us we'll see her again
Whenever our earthly time is done.

(For Dierdre)

War for Peace
(Operation Enduring Freedom: The War on Iraq)

Our troops are fighting a war for peace
In a distant, foreign land,
Risking their lives for freedom
Of a country needing our hand.

Our President made a difficult decision
To deploy brave women and men,
Knowing some would not return
To loved-ones and close friends.

We watch the news and hear of their fate
And all we can do is pray
That God will keep them in His care
And guide them along the way.

We cry for those we've only known
Through media or family and friends.
We weep for those we've loved and held
With their deaths we must now contend.

God help us know what we must do
To reach out to those in pain,
And help us believe this conflict will
Result in the world's greater gain.

As long as others live in fear
Without freedom, liberty, or peace,
There is little hope for us to feel
That our own will never cease.

There is an inter-connection
Of all that God has made.
Who we are and what we do
Is never an even trade.

While some have more and others less,
Within each heart and mind,
We're gently guided by His hand,
All creatures of one kind.

"...We Got Him"
(Saddam Hussein Captured)

"Ladies and gentlemen, we got him!"
Are words we've waited to hear.
After months of fighting and dying,
And living in constant fear.

As Administrator Bremer broke the news
There were sounds of joy and cheers.
We had captured the man who brought suffering and
pain
Reigning in terror for 23 years.

His people immediately took to the streets
To boldly dance and shout.
Saddam Hussein was finally captured
They knew this without a doubt.

Saturday morning, December 13th
In the year 2003
Is a day of fate for this deposed dictator
That will live in infamy.

Although this gives us reason to rejoice
We must not retreat or quit
The Coalition must prevail
For the whole world's benefit.

The Columbia Seven

They were people just like us
Who had a dream for life.
Endeavors they all knew would help
To save our World from strife.

Their reach was so much higher than
Any imaginable grasp.
So far beyond the skies unknown
And such a formidable task.

They left behind sad families
To grieve and hold them dear.
Who also know, within their hearts
That their loved-ones are always near.

What inspiration can we take
From these seven brave souls?
We must find hope and fortitude
As our own dream unfolds.

Kalpana, David, Laurel, Michael,
William, Rick, Ilan –
You're remembered in our hearts and minds
As you explore the greatest beyond.

Farewell to Mattie

I feel as though I'VE lost a kindred
Spirit from this Earth.
I never met you Mattie
But I certainly know your worth.

I watched you on the Oprah show
And read your poetry, too.
Through it I gained a true sense
Of the tender, loving you.

I was moved by your courage
And positive looks at life.
Even though your physical self
Was filled with stress and strife.

Your heart songs became a comfort
As I read them through and through
They helped me look at life
From a different point of view.

I'll REALLY miss you, Mattie –
A gem, a jewel, a pearl;
I'll think of you quite often
As you look down on our world.

Each time I read your poetry, now,
I'll be reminded of your heart,
And all the songs it gave us
So we're never really apart.

So long, Mattie...

Farewell, Whitney

She was given the gift of a voice for songs,
To uplift, praise, and inspire.
She gave us all that was given to her,
Fulfilling our hearts' desire.

She encouraged even the very young,
As well as the oldest ones,
To pursue their wildest hopes and dreams,
Enjoying life while having some fun.

She was once so innocent and pure,
Gaining experience along the way.
As she grew into her own womanhood,
She faced obstacles every day.

Whatever was placed upon her life,
She moved through it with His grace,
Knowing one day it would all be over,
And she would have her own special place.

Then up, up, and above it all,
An Angel ascended into His Great arms.
He welcomed her, as we bade farewell.
She'll suffer no more hurt or harm.

Thoughts on Hurricane Ivan

I've never seen such devastation
As Ivan brought to us.
I've never seen such hurt and pain
Despair and disgust.

So many families lost so much
So little from their lives retained.
Homes destroyed, roads washed out
Damaged schools among the remains.

Shelters ruined, hospitals touched,
Security compromised;
Our comfort level tested and
Our beliefs are now revised.

For years and years we've lived our lives
In a state of silent denial –
"Not us", we thought, never, never would
Such a storm dare to defy us.

We've lived our lives somewhat sheltered --
Safe and secure -- we knew it.
It's now been changed, for better or worse,
It's our choice how we view it.

We've been given a second chance
To make and get things right.
Another storm will surely come
No matter the day or night.

We must believe that we were spared
For some particular reason.
We must begin to live a life
With a purpose for every season.

In Your Memory (2011)

We celebrate your life today
For what would have been 67 years.
From 1944 to 2007 --
We remember you through our tears.

We also have some smiles and laughs,
For all the good times that you brought.
So we couldn't let this day pass by
Without honoring you in special thought.

(R.I.P Helen Barrow Bellanger)

Remembering

I've seen the way some loved ones
Adjust to our demise.
For the first few days or even months
They keep tears in their eyes.

As the years begin to pass,
The hurt and pain will ease.
They go along their merry ways,
Doing just as they please.

On the anniversary of our deaths,
They take time to recall
The good (and bad) times that we had,
And the experiences of them all.

We can't begrudge survivors,
That we leave behind on Earth.
We know that we will meet again
As part of the divine rebirth.

Coping With Life and Death

Another precious family member
Has gone to meet our Lord.
And as the time goes passing by
We'll adjust to being apart.

We'll hold the precious memories --
The good times and the bad.
We ask the Lord to help us cope
With feelings both happy and sad.

We think of our own mortality
And try to live our lives
By giving the very best we have
As He allows us to survive.

Carrying them within our hearts
We'll know they gave their best
While preparing for our own eternity
When we are called to rest.

From Earthly Life To Heavenly Peace

He placed me in an Earthly body
And gave me a mortal existence.
He directed me the ways to go
And ensured a measured persistence.

Sometimes I feel I suffer so
At the hands of forces unseen.
And yet I know I am protected
By a Father on whom I can lean.

We all know that, at some point,
This Earthly life will cease.
How encouraging for us to trust
We'll then live with our Father in peace.

As long as I live upon this Earth,
My purpose is clear to me.
My acts, habits, and accomplishments
Are all open for Him to see.

Poems About Purpose

> "As far as we can discern, the sole purpose of human existence is to kindle a light in the darkness of mere being." -- Carl Jung
>
> "You are not here merely to make a living. You are here to enable the world to live more amply, with greater vision, and with a finer spirit of hope and achievement. You are here to enrich the world. You impoverish yourself if you forget this errand."
> -- Woodrow Wilson

Make Your Own Garden

You must make our own garden
However it grows;
What it will produce
Only God knows.

Until the sun rises,
And blooms start to appear,
Keep tending your garden,
Year after year.

Each day, give it love
And nurture it, too.
Its fruit will bring bounties
And rewards just for you.

Keep tending your garden
And it will do well.
How strong it becomes,
Only you can tell.

Always remember,
That which you give,
Comes back many times,
For as long as you live.

A garden that is beautiful --
Full of life and good deeds
Is what you must strive for
When planting your seeds.

Keep Dancing

Dancing is living
And life is a dance.
With each step you take,
You're taking a chance.

The music you hear
Is what helps you keep moving --
Fast or slow,
Hopping or just grooving.

As long as you listen,
The rhythm won't stop.
Whatever the beat,
It keeps you on top.

The world is your stage
For the performances you'll give.
Make each one a better one
For as long as you live.

Life's Purpose

If I can know I've changed the world
In some small means or measure;
And others see my constant efforts
As a legacy to treasure;

I'll know I've served a purposeful life
That the Good Lord so intended;
And when I leave this earthly existence
No one will have to defend it.

Think of me as one more soul
Who saw the message clearly;
And reached out most faithfully
To touch each heart so dearly.

Try to find a Point of Light
Shining brightly on your good deeds,
As one of God's most special ones
Reaching out to those with needs.

I Believe The Lord Places Us

At times we think our life's not fair –
We pray and ask for reasons.
And wonder why we suffer so
Throughout each and every season.

The answers to our solemn prayers
Lie within our realm of trust
That through it all we realize
The Lord always places us.

I believe the Lord places us
Wherever He wants us to be
At any given place or time
Revealing what He wants us to see.

I believe the Lord places us
To accomplish His special deeds.
He lets us know, without a doubt,
He will fulfill all of our needs.

I believe the Lord places us
To experience some good and bad.
He also helps us, by His will,
To know both happy and sad.

I believe the Lord places us
Where we grow in every way –
Knowing that His hand is there
At every point throughout each day.

I believe the Lord places us
To bend but never break,
Just like the mighty palm tree
Giving us no more than we can take.

And when He's done with placing us
Down here on His green earth,
He faithfully brings us home to Him
To experience our grand re-birth.

My Secret Name

I've always known I have a purpose
Down here on God's green earth.
I knew the work He had for me
Would ensure and seal my worth.

Then I discovered, just recently,
I have a Secret Name.
It's known only to the Lord above,
And it wasn't just some game.

In time He revealed the name to me
I was to be called "Inspire"!
This was sweet music to my ear
And it met my heart's desire.

Our Purpose Here On Earth

If I have touched just one,
My purpose is getting done.
Another two or three or five,
And I'm feeling quite alive!

If those I've touched touch others,
The purpose shall continue.
It doesn't matter the number,
The scope, location, or venue.

The World is ours to change,
Making it a better place to exist –
Not only for us, right here and now,
But for those who will persist.

Our purpose on this Earth
Should be clear – but it's no small feat.
We exist to make some difference here
In the lives of those we meet.

Be Who You Were Meant To Be

No one can determine who you are
Or change what God meant you to be.
Search your own heart, mind, and soul
So you can clearly see.

God creates us all for a reason.
This is His means to express
Our individual uniqueness,
Which allows us to pass His tests.

The human form is only the shell
To protect what He placed inside.
The true gifts and talents given to us,
Are the things we cannot hide.

Purposeful Life

There comes a time in all our lives
When we just want to please
Our family, friends, and others,
Or we feel ill-at-ease.

In later years our quest is
To be whom we were meant to be,
No matter what others say or do
Or what they seem to see.

For we were made to follow
Meaningful, purposeful lives --
Not only for ourselves and others
But for next generations to strive.

Poems About Family

My Mother, My Rose
Our Firstborn
Missing You
The Hole Grows Bigger
A Special Father
Fathers – Near and Far
Always Near, In Our Hearts
I Still Get To Be Their Mom

My Mother, My Rose

A Mother's love is like a rose
Whose scent lingers with her offspring,
Reminding them of her petal-soft heart,
Protective thorns,
And long-lasting beauty.

Our Firstborn

Mommy and Daddy are very proud;
Shouting happy, shouting loud.
Took your time but finally made it;
Now we know just why you waited.

Curly hair and Daddy's mouth;
Big brown eyes and Mommy's pout;
Perfect fingers, tiny toes;
I think you've got your Mommy's nose.

A head so small and round, I see;
And little ears fit perfectly;
A smile upon your little face --
The gift of life, so full of grace.

You were sent from heaven, above
For us to have and hold and love.
We've waited very patiently
For your arrival, finally.

And now we'll hold you in our arms;
Feel safe, sweet baby, free from harm.

Missing You

There's a little hole in my heart,
Growing bigger every day.
It's there because I'm missing you
Since you went away.

I try so hard to fill my days
To help set aside the pain.
But no matter how hard I try
It just seems to be in vain.

Don't let this hole keep growing
Without stopping in to say,
—Hello, Mom, I miss you too.
That will surely make my day!

The Hole Grows Bigger

The hole in my heart got bigger
When the next son went away.
I didn't think I could miss him
So very much each day.

Sometimes I sit and think of them
And how it used to be
When they were home and still around
Just Dad, the boys, and me.

These feelings of great loneliness --
Each day they come and go.
Sometimes I'm up, sometimes I'm down
And still I miss them so.

Finding things to do for me
And catching up on life,
Helps to keep me focused and
Relieves a bit of strife.

No matter how far away they are
And no matter what they say
The hole in my heart will continue to grow
A little bit more each day.

A Special Father

Not only a wonderful husband
You are a special father, too.
Our children could not have done better,
If they had hand-picked you.

For all you give to teach them
The lessons they need to know
Your love for them is without limits
As you show them the way to go.

Sometimes it seems so difficult
To get them to understand.
Other times they seem to really see
The example of a strong and gentle man.

The Lord has placed you in their lives
As a special gift to them.
Remember when you provide guidance
It comes directly from Him.

Fathers – Near and Far

I don't know much about what it's like
To grow up with a Dad to hold.
He left this world early in our lives
When I was only four years old.

Although the years after he had passed
Were filled with family love,
There always was an empty spot
Only filled by the Father above.

Still I wish I could have known
Firsthand about my earthly Dad,
Not only from the stories shared by Mom
But from experiences I might have had.

If you were blessed to have a Dad with you
Throughout your formative years,
Thank God that He has given you that
And saved you many tears.

But if, like mine, he left too soon
Leaving you no earthly Dad,
Thank God, the same, despite it all
For being the Father you've always had.

Always Near, In Our Hearts

You'll always reside within our hearts,
No matter how far away.
We'll think of you and love you so,
From the distance, each and every day.

You were given to both of us
To guide you on your ways,
Until you accepted His guidance
To know and receive His Praise.

Always stay in constant touch
Whether you are far or near.
Let us know of your ups and downs,
And we will always be here.

So off you go with blessings from us
To chart your own path in life
Know that we are so proud of you
As you encounter the stress and strife.

Go forth as Young Men, within this world,
Always striving to make it a better place.
Take responsibility for your thoughts and actions,
In whatever challenges you face.

[For Hendric and Westin -- 2014]

I Still Get To Be Their Mom

It matters not how far they go,
Venturing in and out of harm,
God has given me the right and the privilege,
So I still get to be their Mom.

Morning, noon, day, or night --
Even from dusk to dawn,
Whomever they meet, wherever they go
I still get to be their Mom.

Married or single, whatever they choose,
And whether they are excited or calm,
I accept their choices and the state they are in
'Cause I still get to be their Mom.

The love I have given to each of them
Strengthens my heart like the mighty palm.
I send up constant prayers on their behalf
Thankful I still get to be their Mom.

"When one is out of touch with oneself, one cannot touch others."
                    -- Anne Morrow Lindbergh

Poems About Celebration

> *"The more you praise and celebrate your life, the more there is in life to celebrate."* -- Oprah Winfrey

A Very Special Birthday Wish
Thanksgiving Day
HAPPY HOLIDAYS!
As You Leave...

A Very Special Birthday Wish

Reaching this age is a very big deal
-- At least, it is for me --
Because of the Blessings I have been given
And all the things He's allowed me to see.

Whether good or bad times
He's been there through it all
Ever ready to answer
Whenever I call.

He's given me a great family
And wonderful friends
A good job with security
A strong house to live in.

He ensures I'll be fed
And have clothes on my back.
He takes care of all my needs
So there's nothing I lack.

On this special day
I can feel Him in the air,
Saying, "Happy Birthday, My Child,"
"I will always be there."

Thanksgiving Day

Thanksgiving Day is a time to be thankful
For that which we hold close and dear;
A time to reflect on the past and the present,
Family and friends – far and near.

As we partake of good food and cherished company,
Let's take time to remember those without.
They, too, give thanks for any blessings received
And things more pleasant to think about.

HAPPY HOLIDAYS!

The Holidays are so special –
A time for gift exchanges;
For celebrating with family and friends
And making some meaningful changes.

As you go through this sacred time
Please do not neglect
To remember the true reason we celebrate
And give Him due respect

As You Leave...

For all that you have done for us
And all the times we've shared
We couldn't let you leave us
Without showing how much we cared.

Another time, another place
A new journey, another quest --
Keep in touch and think of us
We wish you "All the Best"!

"If you say what you think, don't expect to hear what you like." -- Malcolm Forbes

After Word

I truly hope you have enjoyed reading this inspirational poetry as much as I enjoyed sharing it. It is my sincere desire that, after reading these words, you will keep them near and refer to them whenever you feel the need.

As always, thanks for your interest in my creations.

NOTES

www.ingramcontent.com/pod-product-compliance
Lightning Source LLC
Chambersburg PA
CBHW071805090426
42737CB00012B/1958